basmati brown

basmati brown

phinder dulai

NIGHTWOOD EDITIONS

Published by
Nightwood Editions
R.R.#22, 3692 Beach Ave.
Roberts Creek, BC
V0N 2W2 Canada

THE CANADA COUNCIL | LE CONSEIL DES ARTS
FOR THE ARTS | DU CANADA
SINCE 1957 | DEPUIS 1957

Cover design and illustration by Paul Pahal
Author photograph by Jaqui Birchall
Other photographs by Phinder Dulai
Typesetting by Smoking Lung

Nightwood Editions acknowledges the financial support of the Government of Canada throught the Canada Council for the Arts for its publishing activities.
Printed in Canada..

Canadian Cataloguing in Publication Data

Dulai, Phinder.
 Basmati Brown

Poems.
ISBN 0-88971-172-0

I. Title.
PS8557.U385B37 2000   C811'.54   C00-910702-9

dedicated to

Jane, Natasha and Nadya

Table of Contents

c r o s s   a n d   o p e n

glossary

acknowledgements

Exile

Exile is not a new theme but it fits the purpose here. More than two-thirds of this collection was conceived while I was away from Canada, on trips through India. The book was written over a four-year period and went through several title changes and three major structural changes. Chalk it up to growth.

These poems constitute a journey. Poetic ports along a raging ocean. Not places in the concrete sense, but ghosts of memories—familial, political, social, spiritual and sensual. Literally, they offer up many references to the migrant life in Canada, and yet, they speak of home and homeland without nostalgia, and with a clear place of connection—British Columbia.

I have learned in the past few years that it is not healthy to tuck away the lingering spirits which sometimes surge into the printed word. They offer up twin points to the psyche, even numerous spaces. I am comfortable with the soft ground that is left to me, a ground fertile with hybrid possibilities.

We are all parties to our own personal blood narratives; one can never turn away from family lineage. I often wonder if the first South Asian settlers who arrived in British Columbia a century ago had not been illiterate rural Punjabis what our community would have looked like today, and how it may have impacted more on how we view literature in this province. As with all things, time allows for change, and breaking through closed doors is not an easy nor a popular job. A drop in a calm lake is not just a drop, for it always has impact on the rest of the lake. It collects with earlier drops from fifty years ago—voting rights, the right to own land, the right to pursue professions etc., etc.

Compared to my first book *Ragas From the Periphery*, I have dropped a little closer to the centre of the lake. This time around my observations are a lot more personal, so say hello to my family in these pages—they have withstood large waves.

Similar to *Ragas*, these poems commune with language in a spritual/social journey.

As with most young boys in Punjabi households, I was once the server of the drinks at family gatherings while inebriated elders crooned *ghazals* and Punjabi poems and songs that expressed everything from spritual ecstasy to political freedom from the British Raj. Call me a popular metaphor for the *Saki* (wineserver) if you will, but I do hope that I can seduce you with my liquid words and bring you into this home—a Canadian home, a British Columbian home, nonetheless, a Punjabi home.

Welcome.

Phinder Dulai, June 2000

Some of these poems have appeared in earlier versions in *West Coast Line* (*Between South Asias* anthology) and the inaugural issue of *Blissforwomen.com*.

p a t h s

. . . a mother's caress

. . . a father's assurance

. . . was never like this

. . . will never be

caste(ing) a line

a line
"caste"
down
unknown
slippery sheaths of brown

looking down the line
i say
"how my bread breaks
like rock candy"

you say
"sweets are still
all i have for you—
remember to bring
in some grain and corn
the next time you come"

my mother
strong as my stubbornness

said "*mali*, never fear the *goré*
always stand up to them"
mother's line from pasla

a three-level house on a farm
stretching to the crimson gold
never seen angels before until
we drove by them in cotton fields
sometimes land and money
offers you words and language
and sometimes together
they both open the path

my father's line
a few fields, a water pump
dishevelled home
a dark room
haunted by
baba punjab singh's lost soul
marched into persia with no return
sacrifices long forgotten

when dad drove to his bride's village
all loved the american cadillac
to take her home
mom's side gave a sigh of relief
thinking kenya had been good to their family
not knowing the truth

a football cup sits in the storage room
in purttappra
to the captain of the team
when mani singh kicked a ball high for us
it was in memorial park, coventry
we never thought it would come down
laughs fall from a young man aged by expectation
two steps walk—a gallop
then *toushh*—the football in the sky
followed by laughter

brown eyes
dark shading
means
working out of gradations
down the line
caste(ing) the line
not all are *jatts*
not all can be *brahmins* either
and to escape

was to join the army
lie your head to a stone
an imperial defence

down the line
down the line
caste(ing) and classing
farmers and bricklayers welcome

mid-life (for mother)

my gardens have died
i planted roses, lilacs, small ferns, tulips and carnations
goodbye
goodbye
my body rages
i want half the mind back
i want to live in my living room
my babies on the mantle
their eyes changing and changing
years, nights, full moons
coyotes singing
in the fields lining the airport
calling out
crying out
hearing the cessna jump into the sky
cessna rage
let it fly into the wind
loud with my words
and ring out my failures
let everyone know
i do not cry anymore

i want what is mine
half of his soul is mine
bite into it, rip at it
gnaw at the flesh that transgressed me
years squandered by ownership rights
claw back 35 years lost to duty, honour and family pride

my girls laughing
so hard
family visits
displaying ease
with malicious intent

my boys—the loud music
catch it in my hands
blanket my home with it

pain rolls into my body
hanging arms, brittle
cobwebbed fingers
at night i roll my hair down
sometimes my youth looks me in the eye
asks, "what did you do for yourself?"

some nights
my body aches
my flesh prickles with sweat
and phantom hands touch me in dreams
swaying me in raptures long forgotten

let my arms grow
so that i can pull the house,
its roots, take it back with me
let it breathe back into me

mid-life (for father)

to live again
feel the soft skin
hold your thighs around my belly
let my rough fingers bathe
in the soft autumn of your flesh
make them gentle again
give them youth, awaken my veins
criss-crossing my hand and knuckles

my home is a broken voice
drunken voice
surrounded by whispering walls

changed faces
babies turned to adults
a mother lost to bitterness
taking my memory with her
desire frozen in the
clear lake of my burdens
petrified meat on hooks

what i knew before
means nothing today

i cannot speak
hollow words
kiss back the years
passion amidst treachery
a fate of barren destinies
children drifting along and alone
love never spoilt them
allowed them to laugh
deep and full

i have done
i am wrong
a circle runs through it

word play

sing the moment
suture fate
torn out
when you found
nothing
like a
rapturous curve
dark and doughy
the stomach's dimple
my tongue circling
circling
like a fleshy vulture
circles me
over me
and
over me

before you awoke
watching you return
wanting succour
not knowing
how to be
when to be
what was it
you were supposed to be
machine man
phantom tears
laughing without stomach
living in the shadows
on the edges
shredded fingers
yearn for softness
in a permafrost soil
in a home half built

given
a mouth full of filings
and ice
to numb your needs

play the words
as they fall out
mouth shaping
stories
out of icicle landscapes
desolate city highway
singing quietly
hidden in the basement
in the garage
full of junk
a full joker
in a home
anger-brimmed
closed
quiet

silence is gold
across skies full of fury

your quiet
muted the sky
turned fury back
and the world stood
in its tracks
bristling
listening
to rage
as it spilled across
faces not known
when it began

the "due"
grew around you
but never touched your lips
you never tasted it
the dream
the due never yours
the handshake
shaken with others
never given
enveloped in yours
hand/full
two hands
envelope each other
carrying the body
holding together
warming the fingers
twisting the hard skin
scratching the calluses
smoothing the cut
running over cold knuckles
knuckled hand
clasping
hand
holding together
hold . . . it . . . together

sometimes
when the clock
decides to
break the rules

when it stops
brings its hands
together
bidding you *salaam, teri sehat kidan*
and bows its head

i imagine running traces
around the temple
of your weary soul
to calm you
sedate you with my echo
keep you warm
when the night left you dead
in the dark
when the world
said
"no"

canadian, eh! or depends on who you ask!

first class—1965
blighty not good to them
factories and mines
for generations
anger between walls
wars between times
souls like bomb shelters
gardens dug down to protect
but still there because
you know
everything is ruined now
after the two tragedies
made them fake
normal
walls between districts
public vs grammar
office vs mine
souled out by mine
couldn't have
used a shovel
to retrieve what they lost down there
where the air sucked
out hopes
and eyes never saw colour again
black vs white
miners vs "jenall-men"
hardhats vs top hats
and a guinness vs martinis
like paki vs the national front

smoked at 13
lost virginity at 15
wore drainpipes at 16
became a mod

a poor classic
northern frailty
public school sedated
kicked out without reference
no qualification
decided to move across
the atlantic
and settled his unrefined
huddersfield twang
to a starry-eyed
vancouver
a country garden
amongst mountains
and native lands
the english pale
on a foundation of graves

upon arrival
unquestioned citizenship
easing into entry
slow job full of promise
mobile and mutate
english ancestry
once poor and contemporary
now a country squire
now a "jenall-man" on the right side
lapping in
learning to be opportune
trusted and confident
skillful path and stable
assurance to family-built
houses bought and sold
young and wise money
dreams into home
on the nicer parts
create to reconstruct

children
and their place
they love
a nest egg
two birds
quiet determination
live the dream they dreamt
after the horror of birth

. . .

second class—1970
air india to london to toronto to vancouver
jatts—the peasant caste
the poorside landowner
jameen ta thoree ah
the poorer side of the green revolution
par m.a. kithe
english literature master
an education bought by mortgaged land
the first to be someone we are not

punjabi university, patiala
no st xavier's college, bombay
no delhi university degree
from patiala to delhi to embassy
officer: "yes mr singh, canada has need for professionals
like yourself"
while officer-sahib thinks of servitude
good office cleaning staff

pierce the time wall
land on cold earth
entry suspicions
custom direct
red line filled with brown

broken by walls
by walls within walls
while white ones
move to the green line

who are you, why did you come?
we need to verify your identity!
have you ever been convicted of a criminal offence?
do you have any communicable diseases?
your education is not recognized in canada
you must begin again

basement suites, babies already! babies
your fault for coming here
begin again
chitti for *bharat*
risthidar expect canadian dollars
to pay for your education
employment counsellors and welfare officers say
work now, educate later

opportunities in the service sector
do you know how to drive?
how about cleaning?
the mills always hire "your kind"

street lamps
strike over eyes
emptying out garbage cans
auden and spender remembered
spelt out the
tyranny of the past
on an ineffectual present
wrapped and insinuated itself
around the invisible
the sleeping poor

and ran a choke hold

four years and a test
citizenship officer: "who was the first prime minister of
canada?"
translator: "uncleji, where do most punjabis go to eat a
chicken burger?"
"mcdonald"
canadian
eh!   or

canadian
double shift nightmare
shape shifts into grey
wife latches on,
holding her ground
one day
after adding up all the double shifts
holidays and weekends
bought the rest of the house
on the wrong side

· · ·

canadian eh—1999
shape shifter loses sight
lost feelings
danced on the edge
and became numb from the inside
watching children speak
in english

confusion
canadian eh!
canadian

all inclusive

i'd like to take the package
a job
pay for my work
hired not fired because i'm brown
stability
to keep my kids warm
let them run while their air
is still pure
before they learn the anger
the rejection, the betrayal
holiday pay
kindness
to dance with my girls
on a hot evening
in a hot place where
beaches smile

move on, they say

move on
like induced amnesia
don't remember it
get on with it

move on
like cutting off your hands
when you wrote about it
only to be given
hands that don't fit
feelings that don't sit
songs that don't skip
the way you remember them

move on
onto what?
like i dont know you
you don't know me
we never fought
and you never called me it

move on
like the car
full of miracles
thank goodness
we got through it
move
let's move out of this
dump
get a better place
when your pain
stayed
and has never let you go

move into smile
like i smile because
the world's a great place
or because great places
never invaded me
my mind
time
and i forgot who shit
on me all these years
like i don't remember

move on
you made it
it made you fucker
fucked you good
and when your babies
were poor
and your beloved
lost sight of you
and you had nothing
but rage
you smiled to the world
and smiled
and smiled
and smiled
and everyone thought
because you smiled
you were
okay!

move on
forget
mama's
writhing face
palpitating, twitching with anger
full of fury

unable to name it
blame it, shame it
or stake a claim on it
because there were only kids
and only an angry dad
forget dad
chains
telephone wires
phoning up the bosses
out of a ripped-up book
begging, pleading
kissing for a job
rendering life in two minutes
while foremen laughed to themselves
"taut" the bull broken
barren dreams
fateless faith
thank you

move on
take the tour
buy the holiday
all inclusive
buy nothing
the new life
comes with one low price
your soul

move on
when they
carved you out
put the mark on you
and now say
good, you made it
time to move
get in line

with the rest of the bastards

MOVE ON, they say

MOVE ON, they say

MOVE ON, they say

MOVE, they say

MOVE, they say

MOVE ON . . .

MOVE ON . . .

MOVE ON . . .

move

basmati brown
(confession of a punjabi breeder)

i'm coming out
i shall say
i'm outing my self
declaring:
hey, and by the way i'm brown baby
and though i know the
low (g)lass achievement
will not change
i want the world to know i'm brown
like a dark cup of coffee
dollops of cream
lots of succour
dark green brown
an oak tree in full bloom
marigolds ripple with velvet flesh
an instant when you squint
hues exploding into each other
in glorious fluidity

i want you to know i'm as brown
as the earth that once shaped the way my mother ran
how she whispered of her life, future and husband
thinking that he would be the oldest and wisest
when she knew she would have to be the oldest and wisest
in a new land that ate up dads 16 hours a day
stumped out souls
no wonder she lost her mind
a child's mind, wise beyond her manic laugh
that still raised five kids
sits broken
like a raggedy doll
doing time in the playhouse
wondering

where did they all go
and laughs when her punjabi radio station
allows her sometimes to phone in
and offer the world her views and thoughts

i'm basmati brown, feeding into you into me
as silver streaks, and glory follows me
folding around
a ghostly cloth
dirty with age
maybe an outline
the bearded one
saviour as you called it

and the world listens
to the way my foam
reaches the shoreline
and vanishes into the roots of the sand

i'm coming out
through the rail that hugs
dry sediment
when it dies out from under
the tracks, while a line changes
a brother
at the cpr
switches miles
thinking maybe that mile
could bring him someone who will fix him
i'm brown and broken

. . . i get
. . . the job
. . . done

love
i'm broken, don't know how to fix me
fixed me
frozen in the blistering heat
i'm broken
let me be right
open me up
the way i opened
i had friends and soul,
i knew how to love between lines
enemy/friend
a clock turns heavy in my heart

i want to declare to the world
it will mean nothing to say this
cause it means everything
when i out myself to my beloved
she will tilt her head and say
"i know already, i know already"
and i will say
i never knew how brown i was
until i saw it in people's faces
cool amusement
asexual nighttime tryst of fear and lust
curse and cradling head
lines of fixation
oh how brown
fevered paws in the dirt
vats full of strawberries and blueberries
broken smile
brow fretting upon brown
not so pretty eh?
wife beater
illiterate
dirty
small

limited corporate mobility
too good of an employee
shitty worker, does nothing
doesn't even speak english
too smart for his own good
better keep an eye on that one
a real r-a-d-i-c-a-l, shit disturber, activist
shit like brown the way you shit
stinks of curry
should put on deodorant
funny how he doesn't wear a turban, i thought they all did?
hey how come you don't wear a turban?

brown baby,
brown like the *pind*
the way the cow shits it out
life . . . matter . . .
all life matters
but it is nothing for me
to say this
and everything for you

canadian plus

a 79 frost in heathrow
five am travel
pools of ice
bundles of cloth
bistra, rejai,
sarees, kurta pyamas,
guru granth sahib
in the centre
gifts for the relatives and sponsors
all wrapped in clean bedsheets
to carry over to the greener side

black-and-whites from the 60s
young faces surrounded by babies
contours not known, lines not seen
anguish never heard in smiles
affectations for a knowing camera
eye up to confusion
daddy looking deep from the abyss
mama smiling into dreams
our souls
aiming across the atlantic
touchdown
a blind settlement
inadequate
"blue-blooded punjab"
some call us
for not being the wretch
they want us to be

a st norbert winter
frost on my nose
chill in my veins
spits in my back

back alley taunts

hard labour
paper routes in late teens,
wendy's in college,
hot dogs
dishwashing to feed children
parking lots for poetry
mcdonalds to make ends meet

moderate academic achievement
the wrong path
no llb, phd, md, mba
broken journalism
chiselling words,
maybe farming them
"straight from india eh?"

collision
no volley, no return
i'm tired, i'm tired
a circled silence

dishwasher

i do things well
on time
appropriate dress
black shoes, a clown's costume
checkered like my life

first the steel, the cutlery
arrange them all
spoons, knives, forks
butter knives, dessert spoons
soup spoons
arrange
mini green crates
patterns, one into another

send them through at 300° c
water!
on a break
eat the benefits
pasta sauces, chicken breast
looking around
wondering
declarations
by student waiters
on the right path to the right break
and waiting for a bit extra
without asking you whether
you are one too

back to the pit
water machine
where fine white hands
carry clean cutlery
from brown raw hands

wrinkled and dirty

if asked
where are the dishes
i say "sohrry, noh sahpeek dhe inglesh"

p a s s a g e s

. . . backward

. . . land towards

. . . the noise

. . . between whispering gods

. . . heaven bound

. . . the eternal music

. . . and walking

The Howrah Suspension Bridge crosses the Hooghly River, the main river artery through Calcutta.

The Writer's Building is one of Calcutta's heritage buildings, used by British civil servants during the days of the British Raj. It now serves as the municipal buildings

hooghly river haze

backdrop
battered high rise . . . n
from angry words
packed between bricks
heavy with dry blood
caked with *paan* blood
smeared with urine
and a leftover wank

shooting up
grab to the quiet cry
insane incessant night
speaking with machine tongue
honk word
intersect
with wounds and bullets
victorian ghetto
indigenous
to clay rising
high history
brittle bashed zeal
old myths alive
warp the known
ground out whispers
tenants out of owners
owners out of visitors
building
the mirror of one's skin

backdrop
eyes
crevice wrinkle curled
under chocolate brown
down the gully

gnarled fingers
reaching out
old martyrs
line each grid
angry authority
quiet with time
stale victories
acrid rule
murderous polity

backdrop
poets lacerated by historic words
keeping time droplets
artist 'n raging canvas
charcoal smouldering body curves
the lift of wrist, cupped hands
shaping v between thighs
neighbour to fights and failures
harrowing testimony
city cryscapes
only the soul will hear
but never the ear

backdrop
the writer's building
taking word
teaching word
word for conquer
to secede
fingers to executioner
but keeping your head
backdrop
bridge
smog smeared
dangle over
holy hooghly waters

faintly calling out
the city of . . .
bending closer
iron rust dripping belly
waves golden brown
foolish gold
cable
running triangles across the river

backdrop
between frowned smile
sorrow drowned
feeding renaissance
blind trust
encased in peeling blocks

mortgaged off
re-vamped, re-camped, re-sampled, and re-framed
over and over and over
again
dry voice
scream if you can
your children creep amidst the blistering heat

road talk

connect wheel upon
wheel

one way
in the morning haze
another way
in afternoon dust
two ways
for the dark diesel blanket
wheeling and reeling
from the core
calcutta
a century's lapse
plays heritage with a small "h"

four roads meet

shakespeare sarani to carmac to middleton to chowringee
artistic irrelevance
without words
walk the street
cracked
leather face
be hideous and happy
hands hollowed out
the next day's promise
may fill

paan blood runs
around fingers
under the first and second line
of your intricacy
mehndi words
tear-dry eye
coal-dark socket
on an empty face

sudder street's diaspora

rabbi's son
plays on sudder street—circa 1949

son of a rabbi
caste on a ship
without ties to *bharat,*
not *brahmin*
they say crows never leave their homes
and the ghosts of the crows remain
to sing through rustling leaves

israelite
returns to listen
crows
gargle songs
a step backward
clicks on cobbles clean and shimmering
footballs against walls
streets against black rails
railings circling heavy cement
skyward reproducing moses' city

the promised land stripped him clean
sent him to the border
head full of homelands
a 32-year promise
worn down enemies
no man's land
a sentence haunts
the desert
oblivious
echoes words
from hearts burst in battle

the cane
tracing poems backwards
down st sudders
on streets looking downward
hands outstretched, heads looking down
an evening prayer
while *bharati* buildings look in all directions

everything in faces

rastafarian hair
dreadlocks
between naval rings
chin nostril around the cheek stud

afros with pale faces
french, czechs, polish, russians,
americans,
kibbutznik israelis
swaddled together
in gusty house bakery
one long table made from random designs
interwoven
to speak the same language
european

on the far side
persian men
indian men
collate
oblivious chatter
made marginal
shifting continent
power
reflects through
the centre stage

it should be like this
dominant
becomes anonymous
stands out
in back street bazaars 'n restaurants

styling youth
yippie for a new generation
running out of currency
cutting back on food
but keep the smokes coming

when you are home, do you tell
the family your stories, the real ones,
desperate packed-up mules
at tables
or is it the "look what
i bought there for nothing" story

"the bollywood films
are so colourful and funny" story

or learned a few words
namashkar, namaste, and *ick, doh, tin* . . .

could you say
i have found nothing in bazaars
i have found everything in faces
silent with words
loud in their language

citizenship reversed

"but really, you are indian, no?"
padded question

if i say yes
a smile reply:
"you are no better than me" smile
canadian!
okay sir:
indifference
from mutual bitterness

"i don't know"
a chuckle
for contempt

being indian in india:
back of the line
stretching a block
around restaurants
crying out in neon-*angrezi*
"we are number one authentic"

end of the line
wait
weight
out the cost

being *n.r.i.*
is being told home much we
missed
when we fled to blind alleys
unknown
but dark and absorbing

paharganj market, new delhi

guest house to street house
to lay house
to long-distance house
to e-mail house to
textile house to ornament house
to temple house to mosque house
to cheap restaurant house to *gol guppey* house
money exchange house
to shoeshine house
to cheap sweet shop house
to *dhaba* house
to *autorickshawallas* house
to train station house
to bus station house
to shantytown house
to black money dealer house
to police station house
to hostel house and ymca house
to *taxiwalla* house
to *walla . . . walla . . . walla . . .*
wah!

ghats

when you walk down
the cold steps
remember
to tread lightly
down the poor man's altar
where marriage is made
newborns blessed
families encircled
generations affirmed

here the strain and weight
of wet clothes
have been singing
in the wind
arms of leather
throttle them
smash them against steps leading to the river
rub the lather

through them
cleaning out dirty laundry

offer a quiet word
in their absence
knowing the small
arms and legs
carry souls
even granite cannot break

if you remember
the aquatic arc
trailing from their arms and the ruffled frown
on the forehead
remember
to give five rupees
to a child in the market
for the day has died
the mother is resting
while her child
runs circles in the street

ganesh

if a rock fell on me
i wouldn't be too surprised

i have found elephant
footprints on my journeys
the quiet kafuffle of a cosmic joke
played at my expense

i have heard
the crunching and chewing
of cashew nuts
i have been your night's entertainment

you are right
i deserve it
never take pictures
of elephants in india

little gecko

from underneath the chair
the gecko strikes
mosquitoes, blackflies, princess with black wings beware

surveying the tile floor
the silverfish speeds by
the gecko looks the enemy
in the eye
decides its
food
and sucks back the juice
of another kill
s/he returns to the wall
and regally
looks on the transitory kingdom

two of hearts

in vancouver, i am invisible
in bangalore, i was fêted by a thinker and a humanist
who whispered ideas
as mosquitoes hovered over our heads and *taxiwallas*
wailed for us to travel their path at four in the morning

in mysore, the quiet one
disliked by the local young,
entertained by other canadians,
bundled up a word and offered it as a quiet truth

in hassan, where the sand meets concrete
dry heat kisses your lips without a drop of water
i was the invading north and told by the waiter
to eat my food elsewhere

in the goan resort, another waiter
cannot meet my eyes and my friend
eyes a scene that he knows of about only
in stories and movies like *gunga din*
he is the novelist who takes notes
drinks in the politics of my experience
inch-by-inch my world of
ab-normal-see
becomes his reality
i have dealt him that card

the card left for me
is the two of hearts
i must begin again
re-learn, re-turn and face the world

beach walking

on the beach indians stay in one hotel
europeans stay in the other
english-packaged-industrialized
crosses path with high-cast(ing) industrialist
glancing
both to mutual play
a past greatness
wives lounge for brown skin
one hundred heathcliffs
shuffling up to offer drinks

industrialized indian
discovers their place
feel the new order
run through their veins
looking for white women
to play out their karma vision

a family death, return of ash
that left the earth of the *pind* many years back
now returns to breed life in the corn field

from kalingute beach onwards they line-up
like a hungry elephant smacking down its life
to catch up to the new reality

i sitting cross-legged on hot white sand
watching the sliver of the crab
digging upwards
to surface survey
silence pours out of me
both ways
drown out
muddied thoughts

goa

arrival
a topless german sunbather stares
confused and bewildered at my sight
brown tourist
i take off my top to make her feel better
a hotel check
am i legit?

sauntering back
disappointed
i turn to the rays of light
shame clouds
broken blue eyes
and covers them with a t-shirt
to hide from my gaze

i chug on my kingfisher beer
and slip off my sandals

un/broken english

from *shivaji marg*
to *mg road*
desi invisible
brownie to the white tourist
a fellow *coolie* to the colonized

at the gate of india
i received *puja* from a huckster
i gave him two rupees
i prefer it this way
outside the mahalaxshmi temple
i stood still, listened and did not enter

on madam cama road
i waited at the intersection
which had king george at the centre
circled pale
marbled steps
like lord nelson at trafalgar
except here
surrounded by "ambassadors" and *autorickshawallas*
the king is frozen—
a torture and sentence
to pay for sins rendered
unbroken english

postcard

verbatim, the sign says:
"to commemorate their emperor's first visit: king george"

two beggars asleep
inside, monkeys
dance around them
those selling *puja*, palm reading, photographs,
nuts, larger-than-life balloons
blare out
one-liners
no wonder indians are
so good at business in canada

portable harmonium-clad urchins
sing popular hindi songs to the european tourists
they walk onwards oblivious
onwards . . . and onwards

demure lovers
hold hands lightly
parlay in light banter
waiting for a place to fuck

one woman—four hawkers
surrounding her with promises
music, the portable *dholki*,
bamboo flute, harmonium
the gift of a good postcard
of the gateway of india

in this picture
there are none of the above

The Bangla Sahib
Sikh Temple (above)
is situated directly
next door to The
Young Women's
Christian Association's
(YWCA) Blue
Triangle Hostel
(right).

between a sikh temple and the ywca

four steps touch upwards
matha tek
kiss the marble lightly
and pray for a thousand truths

performing line
sevah
entranced duty
enraptured elder
from the shoe rack
a 24-hour *shabad* and prayer relay
mesmerizes the cornea
his own universe
unfolds
his *sevah* betrays a calamity
here for more
an everyday return
ecstasy in trickles
a *paani* splash
cool drop
let cupped hands
funnel a blessing
pregnant with faith
but empty of knowledge
the knowing
waiting for it to arrive
while rolling *rotis*
or handing them out
holi-righteous colour
lime green over face
shiva blue caked on necks and hands
red-hued hair drifts over the zephyr
between *gurdwara* and the ywca

at night
a hindu beggar
turns over at the bus stand
outside the y
whispering underneath the
songs from the *guru granth sahib*
whai guruji ka kalsa
whai guruji ki fateh
turning over again
with a prayer on his lips
not for *sevah*, faith or purity
to buy protection
make a pact with kismet and karma
and connive survival from the clutch of history
he remains half asleep

the airport

a novelist, a poet, an aspiring writer, all canadians

beno, the aspiring writer
sat at the goan airport
letting the sweat drip
heavy on his brow
as he listened
to humanity
a kingfisher beer
one more
he dropped to zero
while george sipped
nodded his head, took a few sighs,
collecting, gathering debris
a parchment of clarity
and drank one more

i sat, chewed on salty fish
and dripped into mindless hum
let my mind go

and whispered the poetry
of our journey, the conversations
leading up to the past

homeless in india
kind of home in canada
when i really want to be in a *gar*
and experience the *maza* of a cool zephyr
i know that will never be mine

rajhdhani railway express

canadian asks
retired sikh officer
"where from?"

reply: "bombay—
family been travelling
a long time,
whole time
from 47—
originally from punjab"

evade the intent
travelling, walking
i've been walking too
i say to myself

whole time walking
pind, gar
vellayat, pounds,
prairies, canadian dollars
and leather wallets

vancouver
three full seasons
the rush of the fraser
cascading along
mission to maple
to port coquitlam
rushing into new west
penitentiary lands
where silences prevail
and reflections are
forgotten
running circles in the centre

driving tails along to vancouver
reaching out the width
folding into the pacific
dissipating into the expanse

skiing
i've never skied
the sisters
tranquil teacher
over vancouver
asleep when awake
and slumbering when it sleeps

comfortable?
when i see squirrels crawl
the greens of stanley, queen elizabeth and forest grove
i see monkeys
and their families
in the shadow of trees
in the dark corners
of the dumpsters
mocking the raccoons

quiet?
the monkeys may hear

people in vancouver
too quiet for their own good
a conversation on the rajhdhani express

cross and open

. . . when you let go

. . . when skies bleed burgundy

. . . and the crisp mist

. . . is a velvet screen

. . . openin . . . openin

. . . and today

. . . arrival

. . . wet blue and new

ambivalence

raja's indian palace restaurant
vancouver all you can eat
take out vancouver, keep out
in vancouver
stay out

waiter hates serving his own kind
small tolerations (us & himself)
glass smiles from the *lassi* jar
cold affability amongst the
onion and tomato salads
and high manners
wah!
never knew such tricks *bhaaji*
what village, which district
(like we don't know such things)
in bombay the waiters
like serving the tourists

the waiter stares
annoyance ripples his eyes, frowns his forehead
"but sir, the wait will be long,
eat on our lower level, fast service
double quick time"
my answer—"i have all the time
in our world"

non-resident indian envy
leaving the motherland
jumping class and caste
rupees to dollars
but still cleaning
they still there
brahminical, parsi, anglo-indian

ownership rights circling their heads
centuries without and with *angrezi*
while they left our kind
to stay on the fields
never sharing, always building walls

across music, literature and cities
got smart
followed our footpaths
after their cambridge and oxford
after their harvard and berkeley
while we worked in factories,
mills and cleaned offices
arriving
on this "native land"
this canada
proclaiming
more needs to be done for us
stole our voices
studied us like rats
sociological surveys
immigration reports and
enculturation habits—pros and cons
sat on boards and committees saying
those kind are hot-tempered
at times inclined to fanaticism
but tell me, *bhaaji*
who used us as a valley
where two faiths collided
where sheep
turned into wolves
surrounding
unarmed farms
peace ruptured
hate erupted engulfing
us all in the drive to

murderous modernity
hope denied in dark valleys
undermining from the start
and drove us
into the cold
where all we began with are hands, eyes
and memory

canada fed us emptiness
nothing to build life here
greenchains later, farmworkers later
cleaning staff later
before we refused to serve
and were hated for not accepting
death in exchange for living death
when everyone hated our petulance
blamed us for rifts
we said fuck you
voted after independence

in india
punjabi = rural idiot
parsi = eccentric and literary
bengali = cultured, musically refined
urdu = *ghazal* and transcendence
towards the pristine light

or—that we did nothing to build life there

now westerners both
we go to the same restaurant
and offer pleasantries
knowing all those things passed
and say we are both
bhaai, bhaiyo, bhaaji

the railway club

i will sit here
counting up my years
travelling with specials
ales, lagers, creams

who knows
they may make me paler
travel through my skin
make me care a little less
languish in the den of drinks

return again
with no gifts, no evidence
hid everything to carry the world
or something to feed the mind

watch the loud patter
as roads glisten
steaming windows
umbrellas broken and dishevelled
lying in pools
humid and sweaty
i remember
i will . . .
i will remember

i will be here when my eyes are heavy
when skin sags deep and folds
into eternity
watching veins
crowd underneath
my knuckles
life
criss-crossing

circumventing my palm

you see me crowd
over the banister—look into the window
watching my eyes lurch over without pain
but glue sticking over pupils
i shall feel the arms
heavy with soft muscle
drawn down with memories
and colour
the sign that earth moves
over flesh too

i shall watch my
face and skin fold
over the jaw
miles and miles
remembering, i have no war wounds
no scars to say i was there

a cuban rain

just before it comes
ecstasy
in arms dripping
from heat

like a lava flow
slow moving
off the local beach
wanting to become
sand
a swish through your fingers
settles for juxtaposition
jagged edge
sweating rocks
on a fluevian plane

just when it happens
you may catch the young
starting to dance
hands joining
becoming ovals
for the rain
seeps in
to squeeze the water
explode between fingers
mouths touch lightly
under a dripping roof
couch the darkness
become shadow
a nocturnal radiance
steal the kiss
letting the lines between
press into each other
open-mouthed

envelope the other
dance to the crickets
a cool wet sheet
and bodies enfold
to the dancing rain

body

when arches
illuminate across dark waters
rippling and buoyant with desire
your coal eyes radiate
offer day in the
wailing night

soft sound
devotion
carry over waves
call to allah
opens me
you are there
with smouldering voice
tongue beckoning
ashen voice
luring me to your nocturnal forest

and i
the hermit
in the forest
will bend to you
envelope your caress
and fall to the earth
with the shattering of rain

familiar

the soft line
around your thighs

your breath
quiet and heavy
dew in the cress
of your bosom

your hard shoulders
offering up
ridges and sea cliffs
jutting out
against the storm

the silk you
draw down over my face
scratching
the rough brittle
thorns of my cheek

the long fingers
you envelope around
my *tablas* hands
sinewy clay feathers

familiar
familiar
familiar

dance/(dha) nce

the light shuffle
tirkatdhin dha tete te te t e
bring the wrist up
to the moon
curve your hand
around the scythe
and begin:

dhaghe dhindha dhin dhin dha
dhaghe dhindha dhin dhin dha

luminous
silver
caress
night
swallows
music fingers
fingers on the skin
skin to bass
skin to treble
tip to *dha*
dhin to tip
rapturous
around your hip
slapping
taals along your curves
playing *dhas*
into your cheeks
sending
songs onto your navel
flourish
a *dadra tal* cycle
around your waist
tender rivulets

along the inner thighs
and land upon the shoreline

where i dance a different tune

what it means to listen

shards of *qawwalli*
tablas maestros
bea (dhin)g te rhy (dhum) out
i listen
with nadya and natasha
at my side
daddy mimicking badly
nusrat songs—bulleh shah
i remember i carried each one
circled them in my arms
running their small bodies
through the rhythm
held them tight to my heart
mimicking badly
but with purity
i carried them both
as newborns

under her breath
nadya sings: "allah hoo allah hoo—allah is everything"
or "*sajna tere bina*—i am nothing without you"
without knowing what she says
tash hums to the cavernous voices
the wailing music
that left tears in the eyes of the converted
and rapture in the messengers

we are complete
in our circle of joined hands
everything possible
nothing failure
living with them
growing with each other
catching the clapping hands

in our hearts
we pulsate on one rhythm
dancing
smiling at each other
we culminate
with the final soft death
of the voice
we break and i fall on the couch
with their hair in my mouth
and face

exaltations

saki returns
server of burgundy words
offered in cups made of song

"beware *saki's* eyes"
for you will drown in the chasm of the muse
drunk with words
dizzy with desire and longing

for those whose eyes
shine
bodies break from rapturous rhythm
art a fleeting bliss
poetry pours into the faithful
souls end life bitterly

i soar
hearing the dew
fall from your lips

spring arrives in my body
when your voice
rings out and calls to the sermon

my flesh burns
when words fly from your mouth
singing them
with a lingering mist
i am warm
in your words
nurtured
in *tavas*
hot ash
third eye

forged into *ragas, talas, qawwals*

now i am lost
in a forest smouldering with
your lilting voice

i am beautiful
when your utterance
smothers me

i am light
when you clothe
my dark skin
with your resonance

i live
when the *sufi's* breath
escape's your lips

now i am wretched
by your absence
your faith
a spring
a full crop of corn
ancestral lands
jullundhar
and mine a poor farmer's field

words within walls, words across oceans, words across words
broken down . . . awkward fury, spoken peace

i accept nothing
you shall live on the luminous page of the moon,
in the eye of my beloved

i shall sing you out over rooftops
counting the million paths
you brought me to your home
where i never reached the threshold

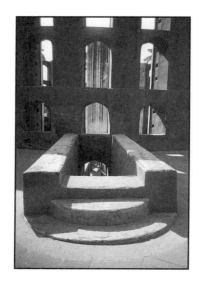

Glossary of Punjabi Terminology

Angrezi—Punjabi, Hindi and Urdu for the English language.

autorickshawallas—mobile rickshaw drivers.

bhaai, bhaiyo, bhaaji—various uses for brother—brothers, brothers, brother. Popular line of rhetoric in Indian political speeches.

bistra, rejai, sarees, kurta pyamas—bedsheets, quilt, women's formal wear, long shirt and Indian slacks (men's clothing).

Blighty—popular colloquial English word for Great Britain that became well-used after the two wars brought urban blight to England's major cities.

Brahmin—the highest caste in India, the keepers of the Brahminical order of the Hindu pantheon, and the purveyors of learning and spritual teaching. In modern India, this elite dominates much of the higher levels of business.

Bulleh Shah—a Punjabi *Sufi* poet.

chitti—correspondence or letter.

coolie—pejorative used for any Indian person in the service of the British Raj.

dadra tal—traditional *tablas* four-beat rhythm cycle popular in northern India.

desi—closest equivalent would be "home-grown," suggesting rural and pastoral identity.

dhaba—roadside eatery, very simple fast food, Indian-style.

dha/dhin/dhin/dha—vocal percussion sounds that form the *taals* known as the *bols*, voice of the *tablas* drums.

Dhobiwallas—collectors of laundry from hotels and residences who perform *Dhobi*, the act of washing.

dholki—large two-sided drum used in Punjabi music and festivals.

gar—home.

ghazal—genre of poetry with aa/ba/ca/da couplets, each one an independent poetic composition meant to be sung and often metaphorically expressing the bond between humanity and god through the relationship of a lover and his/her beloved.

gol guppey—a fried bubble pastry filled with spicy, vinegary water.

goré—pejorative for the "white men."

Gunga Din—one of a number of British films made in the 1940s that is a primary illustration of the British gaze on India. The film illustrates most of the Indian characters as untrustworthy, suspicious and unscrupulous, in addition to lacking any military strategy skills.

Gurdwara—Punjabi for "House of the Guru," the sacred place of worship for all Sikhs.

Guru Granth Sahib—Sikh scriptures and bible.

Holi—northern Indian Spring Festival marking the death of the demon king Holika. Celebrated by lighting bonfires the night before, by performing music all night and by throwing coloured powder and water on people.

ikk, doh, tin—one, two, three.

Jameen ta thoree ah—"My land is a small parcel."

Jatt—Punjabi landowners and farmers—connotes farming/rural stock, and lack of formal education. Associated with the larger Indian peasant caste of Vaisyas.

lassi—cold dairy-based drink made from yogurt, milk and spices.

mali—Indian gardener or security person.

matha tek—"forehead down"—lower your head to the ground and pay respect to the scriptures.

maza—a state of bliss reached by listening to music and being in a moment of enrapture.

mehndi—brown paste used to etch designs on the palms of a woman's hand before her marriage. The designs remain on the skin for a few weeks.

MG Road—nearly every major Indian city has a Mahatma Gandhi Road, in honour of the nation's founder.

namashkar, namaste—Hindi word for official greetings.

N.R.I.—non resident indian—official term used for those who have left India to settle in other countries.

Nusrat songs—the leading exponent of *Qawwalli* music was the late Nusrat Fateh Ali Khan, whose adaptions of *Qawwalli* songs and Sufi poems are considered some of the best.

paan—Indian mouth freshener made with a variety of spices, menthal leaves, betel nut and paste, turns the saliva and mouth red.

paani—water.

par m.a. ketti—"But I completed a master's degree."

pind—village

Puja—prayer ceremony performed by a Hindu priest, a *Pandit*.

Qawwalli music—music originating from Pakistan and Punjab that is a mixture of northern Indian classical music and the poems of *Sufism*, sung by a master of the genre known as an *Ustad*.

risthidar—respected relatives.

ragas—classical Indian music cycles created to illustrate emotional states and based on melodic patterns that reflect certain parts of the day (ie. morning, afternoon, evening).

rotis—leaven Indian bread

Sajna tere bina—"I am nothing without you."

Saki—important wineserver figure in Persian and Punjabi poetry. The *Sufi* poets render the *Saki* as a metaphorical conduit bridging humanity to God through the rapture and ecstasy of intoxication.

salaam—popular word for greetings.

sevah—service to the community and God, figures prominently in the Sikh way of life.

shabad—spiritual compositions performed, sung and spoken in Sikh temples from the *Guru Granth Sahib*.

shakespeare sarani to carmac to middleton to chowringhee—linked up, these four streets (*serani*) lead to the heart of the international part of Calcutta.

Shivaji Marg—roadway that has a statue of the 17th Century *Maratha* ruler Shivaji—one of the first low-caste Hindu rulers to take on both the *Mughal* dynasties and the British.

Sufism—unconventional offshoot of Islam that advocates spiritual ecstasy through music and dance. Closely associated to the *Qawwalli* movement—master singers would perform

Urdu and Punjabi devotional couplets to convert non-believers to *Sufism.* The popular term "whirling dervish" comes from this sect, where dervishes (holymen) become so enraptured in the music and circular dancing, they lose themselves in spiritual abandon.

taals/talas—musical percussion cycles that are the rhythm bases for Indian *ragas.*

tablas—the most popular percussion instrument in Indian classical music, composed of two separate drums - one bass, and the other melodic.

tavas—clay-made ovens found in Indian villages where much of the cooking is undertaken by using dried cow paddies for flame and wood.

Teri sehat kidan—"How is your health?"

Vellayat—Great Britain

Wah!—a common expression given after a poetry recital or musical performance, similar to "Encore!"

walla & wallas—both a noun and a word of action illustrating what a given person does for a living (ie. *taxiwalla*—taxidriver, but more like taxi/bringer/driver).

Whai Guruji Ka Kalsa, Whai Guruji Ki Fateh—"the Khalsa belongs to the Guru, the victory belongs to the Guru."

Acknowledgements

Thanks to my family—Jane, Natasha and Nadya for time given and love extended. They permitted me to travel abroad to attend literary gatherings, where much of this book was conceived and written.

To Sadhu Binning and the other early readers of these poems—big hugs for taking the time out to offer valuable advice and criticism. Further inspirations—Ajmer Rode, Surjeet Kalsey and Rajinderpal S. Pal. A special note for Alan Twigg, who's "cursory" glance (his claim) led to a radical change in the whole look and feel of this book and Howard White because *basmati* resonated immediately with him. Jacqui Birchall for her generosity and good friendship and Virginia Cleary and the BC Touring Council for the Performing Arts for getting my poetry out there.

My many ramblings and "tunings" with Chris Chreighton Kelly netted some great insights and led me further down this book's road, into unknown spaces offering up morsels of light. Thank you Chris.

The Department of Canadian Heritage and The Canada Council assisted me in attending a number of important gatherings in India that furthered my involvement in cultural hybridity and cross-cultural literary experimentation. Roy Miki and Ashok Mathur also supported my trek to the *1999 International Calcutta Book Fair.*

In India, I would like to thank Naveen Kishore and Anjum Katyal of the Seagull Foundation for the Arts for hosting me in Calcutta. Gratitude also to my good friend Parmesh Bhatt and his team at Canada Japan Travel Corporation and to Mr. Azizi at Govan Travels—who quietly muses on Urdu *ghazals* while putting together Indian Tour packages. Thanks to Vibha Sharma and Chandrabhanu Patanayak at the International Centre for the Arts, Culture and the Environment, based in Mysore, India for inviting me to participate at *Convergence 96*, to the University of Mysore and its Graduate Centre for hosting readings during my stay and to Mr. H.K. Kaul at the India International Centre for being a fine host and introducing me to New Dehli's literary journalism community.

In addition, I would also like to thank the Department of Foreign Affairs for assisting me in attending the First International Conference on Multicultural Communication and National Identity: *Challenges and Perspectives*, held at the Universidad de Matanzas (Camilo Cienfeugos), Cuba, where I shared the story of the Komagata Maru to a captivated audience. Professor Walter Temelini at the University of Windsor and Rita Bison at the Canadian Centre for Multicultural Development and Documentation were wonderful hosts—thank you. Cheers to Professors Jorge Louis Rodriguez Morell and Jose R. Congzalez at the university for the numerous Cuban amber rum chats on culture and identity, and a few choice words of poesy. Hats off to Jose, the only English professor I know who can wax eloquent about semiotics, and also do the meanest mambo on the dance floor.

And finally, to Silas White at Nightwood Editions, who pored over details and nudged me along the clear path.